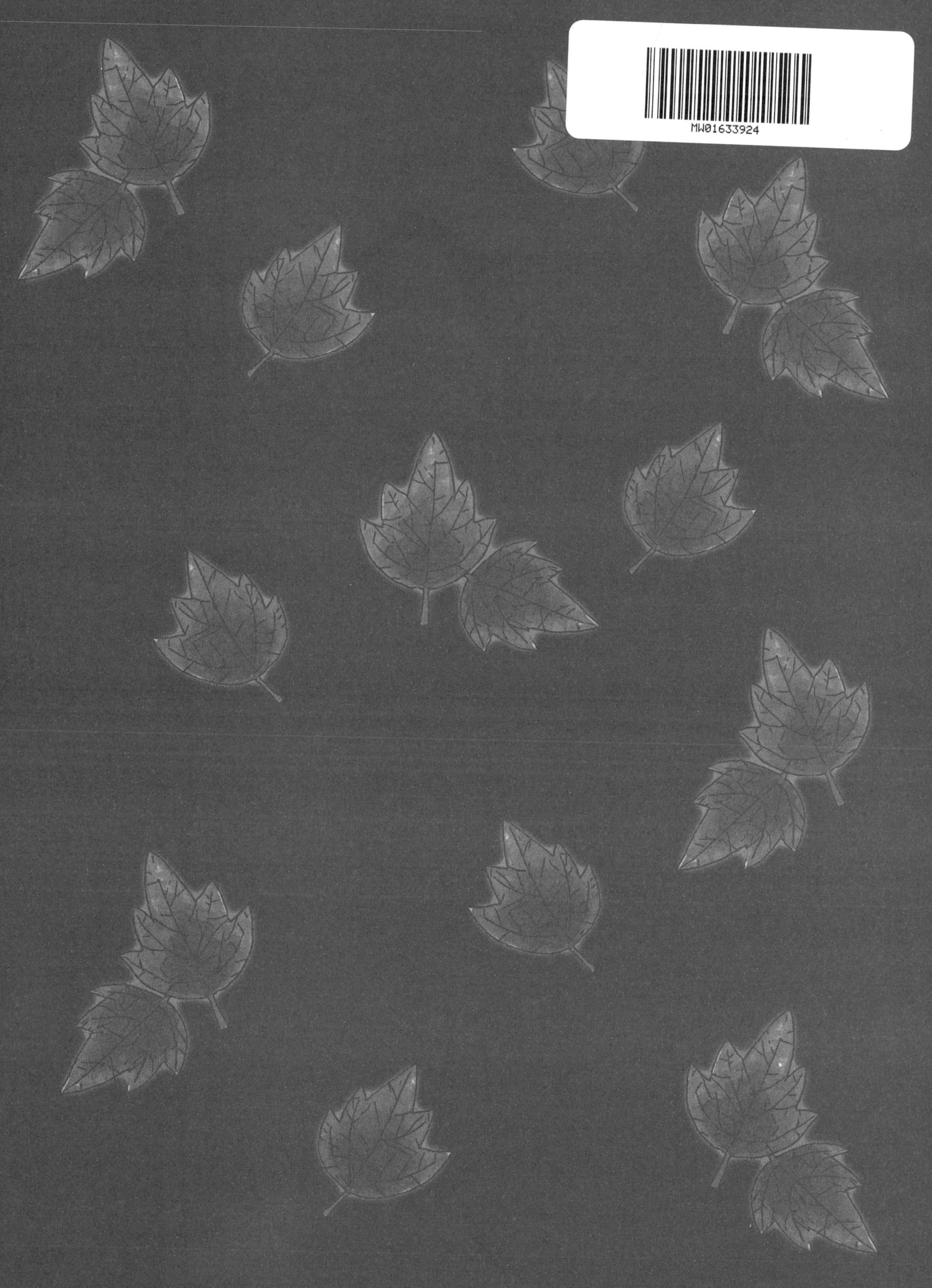

Why does The Raccoon have a Mask?

Story by: Hailey A. Porterfield
Illustrator: Bruce Laborin

This Book Belongs to:

THANKS

Thank you to all my teachers who have encouraged me to write.

I would also like to thank my family and friends for making me feel so special.

This book is dedicated to my mom and grandma for listening to my story and taking it to a whole new level.

Hailey A. Porterfield
6th grade student
Falcon Hill Elementary School
Mesa, Arizona

12

Why does the raccoon have a mask, you ask? The way you will hear this story is from my great-grandma Lucette.

My great-grandma told me that one sunny, bright afternoon the raccoon was warned by the king of all animals.

The king of all animals told the raccoon that if he wasn't going to be nice and friendly he would have to pay the consequences.

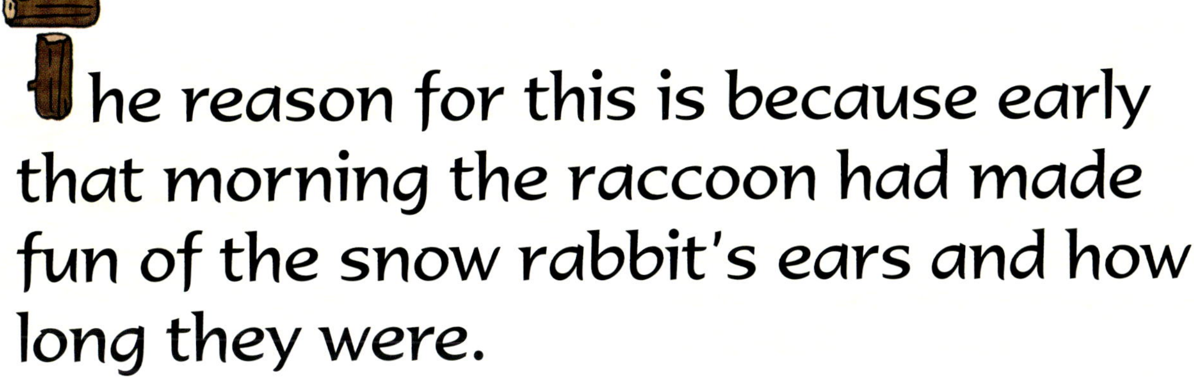

The reason for this is because early that morning the raccoon had made fun of the snow rabbit's ears and how long they were.

Raccoon also made fun of the skunk and how he stunk. PEEEWWW!

Raccoon didn't listen to the king of all animals and went to the snake's home and said, "Oh snakey, oh snakey, where are you?"

SnAKe's
home

SnAke's
ome

Raccoon said, "Catch me if you can," knowing that the snake didn't have arms to tag with or legs to run with.

"Oh raccoon, you have hurt my feelings," said the snake.

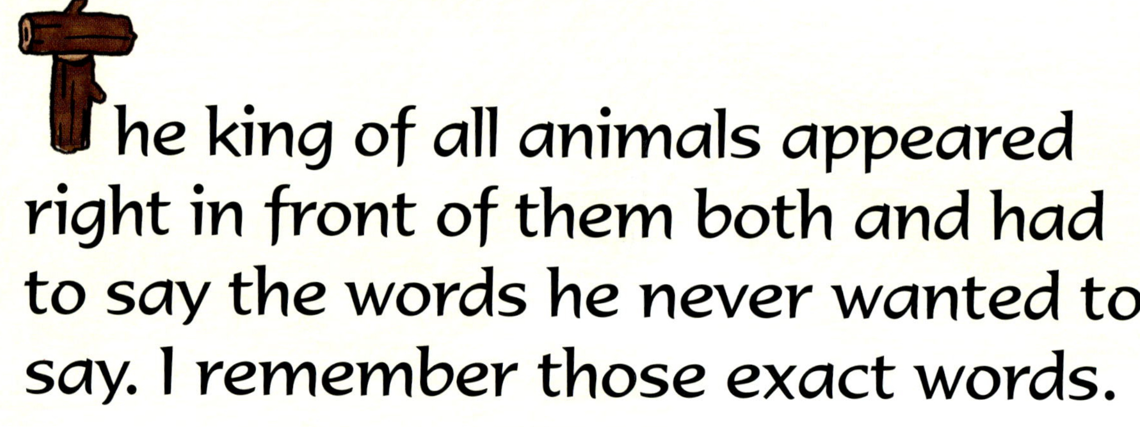

The king of all animals appeared right in front of them both and had to say the words he never wanted to say. I remember those exact words.

"You have disobeyed me, you must pay the consequences. Now you will have to wear this mask forever. You have jeopardized all of the raccoons; they must wear masks as well."

After the mask was on, the raccoon looked different - like with a mysterious glow.

The king of all animals asked, "Have you learned your lesson, oh dear raccoon?"

"YES!" Raccoon said with a smile. "I will behave forever. But if I don't, that's another story."

THE END

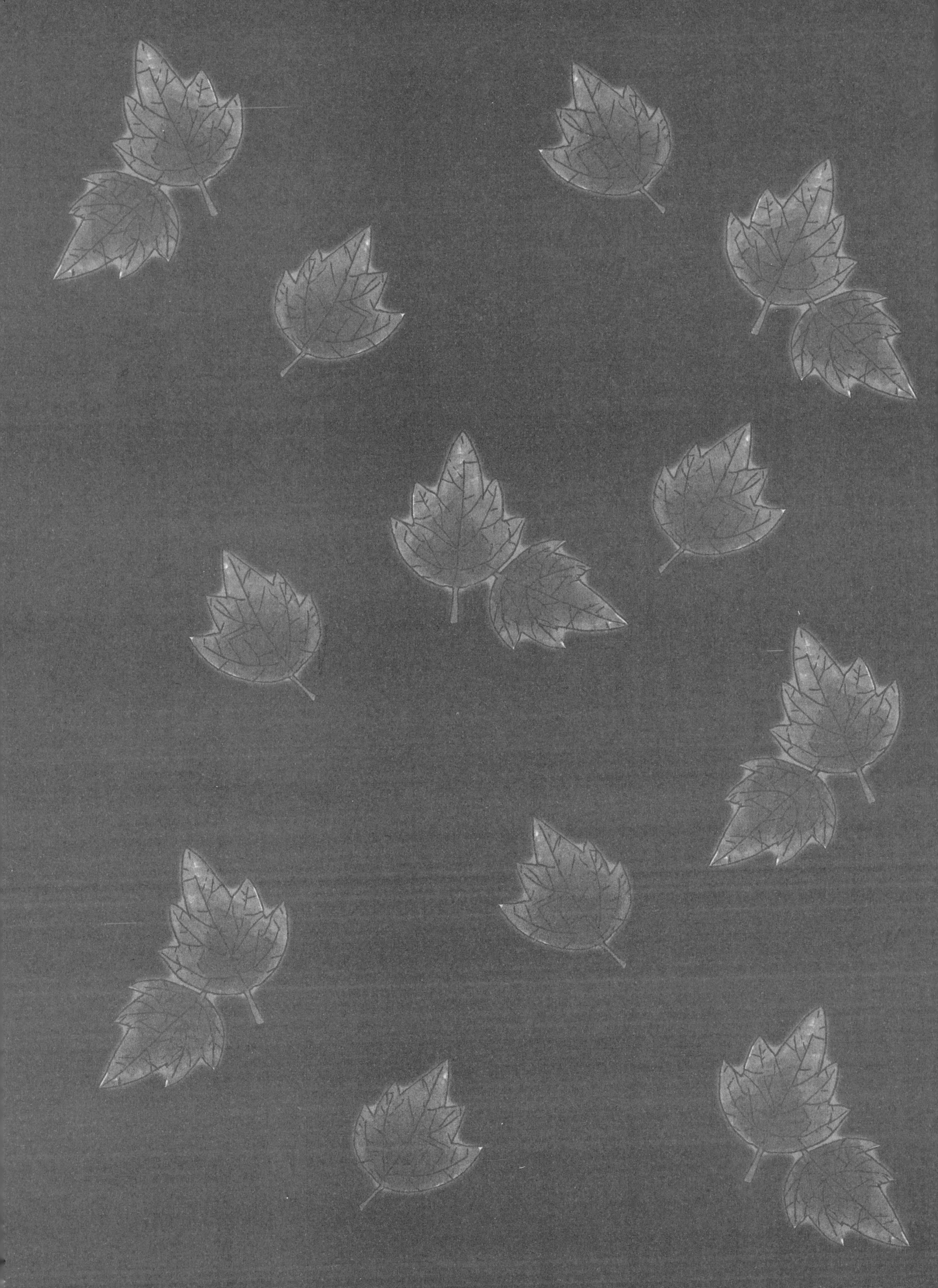